ISBN-13:978-1543174373

Printed in the United States of America

Welcome to a coloring adventure with the Handsome letter H. All these H letters were hand drawn by one artist, Peggy Louise Parrish. She has named them Letter Wonders for a reason. Not only are they unique but subject to transform greatly by you the coloring artist. Depending how you color and fill the detail in can completely bring a new look to her original drawing. Some of the letters inside these pages have examples shown in color. Others are not depicted in color. You may either copy these suggested ways of coloring or completely do it your way. If certain letter designs are especially your type, feel free to make a few in house copies of them to color different ways.

Quality colored pencils are the preferred medium for coloring these pages. However, with a scrap paper placed behind the page feel free to try markers, watercolor pencils , ink gel pens or paints if you want to. The way you color these letters makes each letter part of an extended family of Letter Wonders.

Please leave the artist initials PLP on each design. Feel free to write colored by underneath and make one copy of your colored work.

The Handsome Letter H

COLORING BOOK

By Peggy Louise Parrish

C. 2017

Handsome Letter H Welcomes you to explore

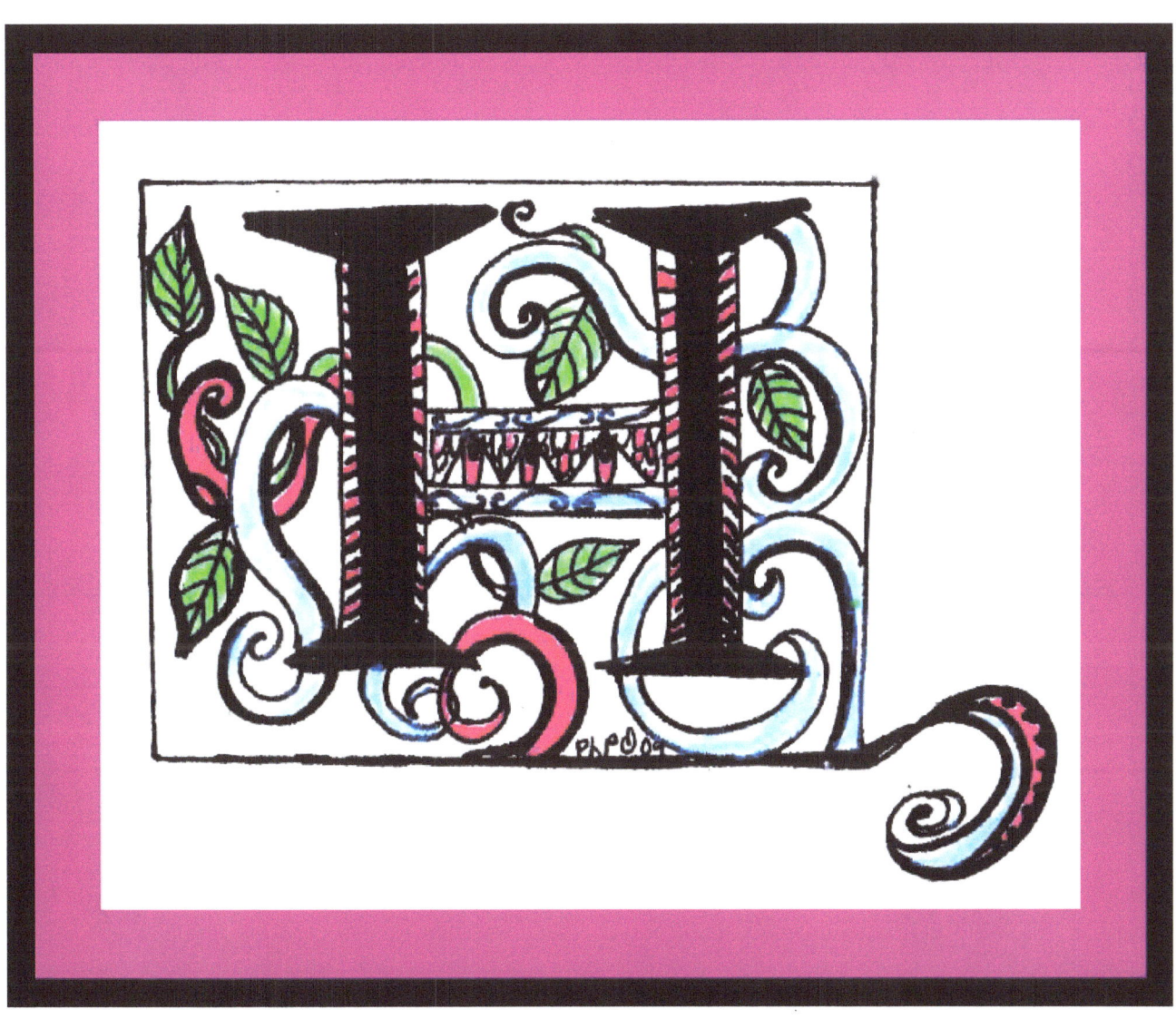

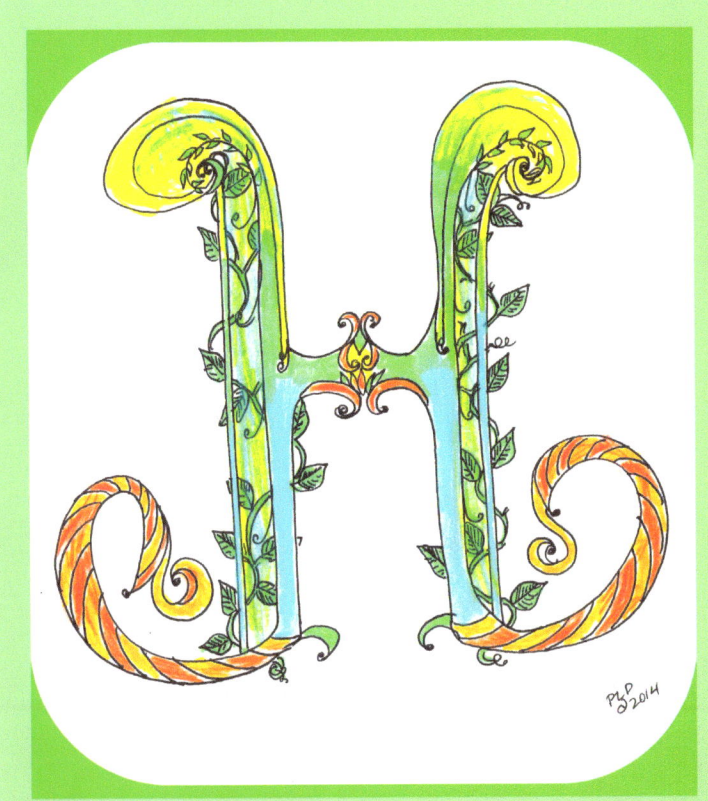

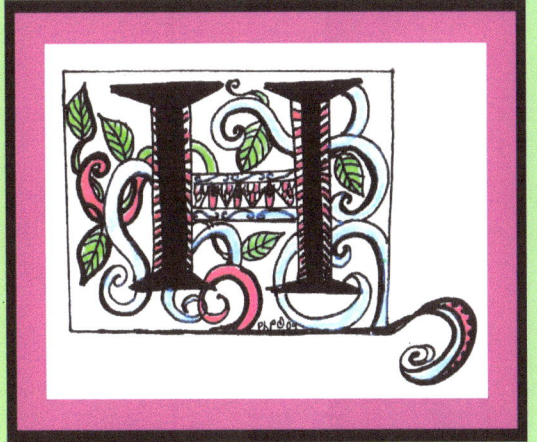

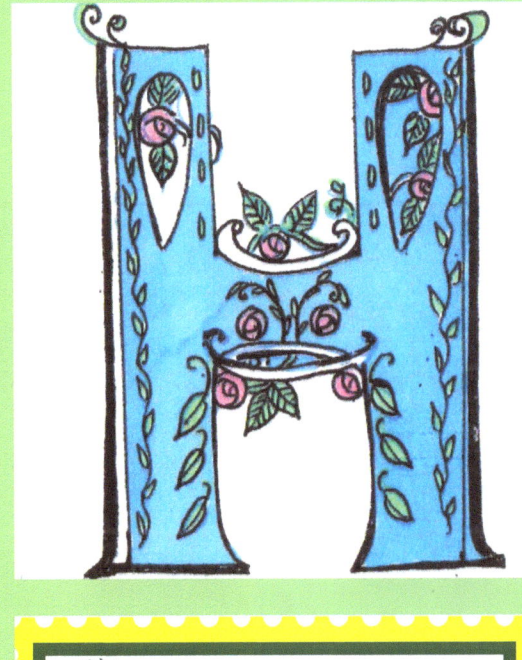

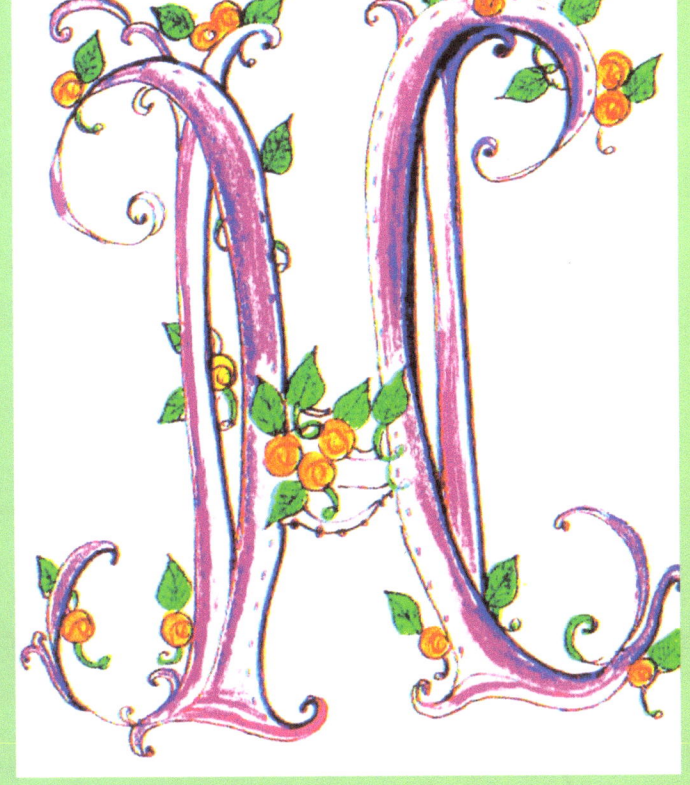

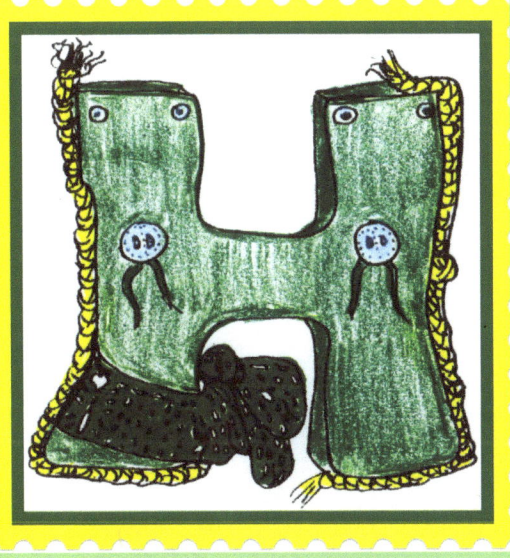

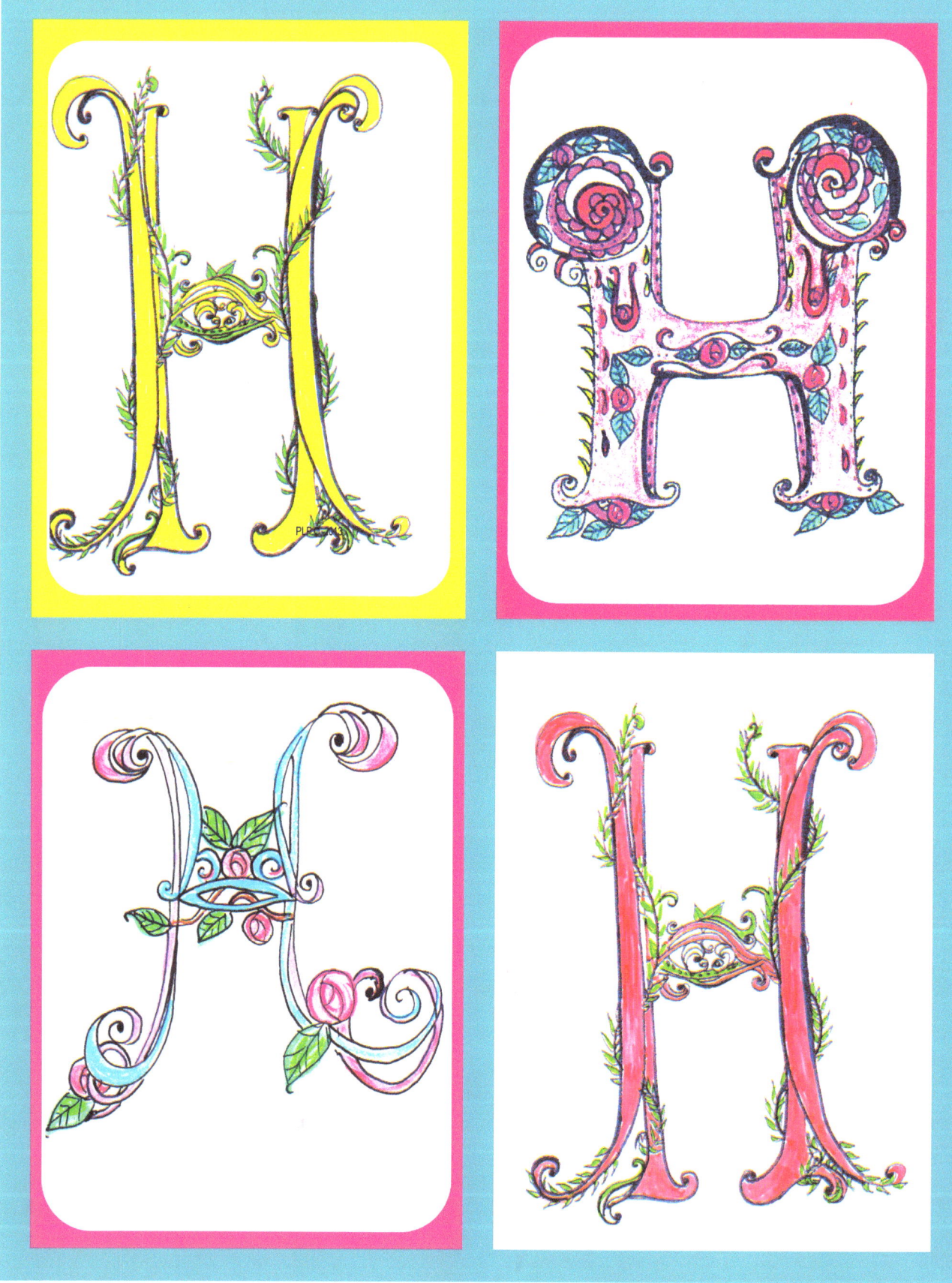

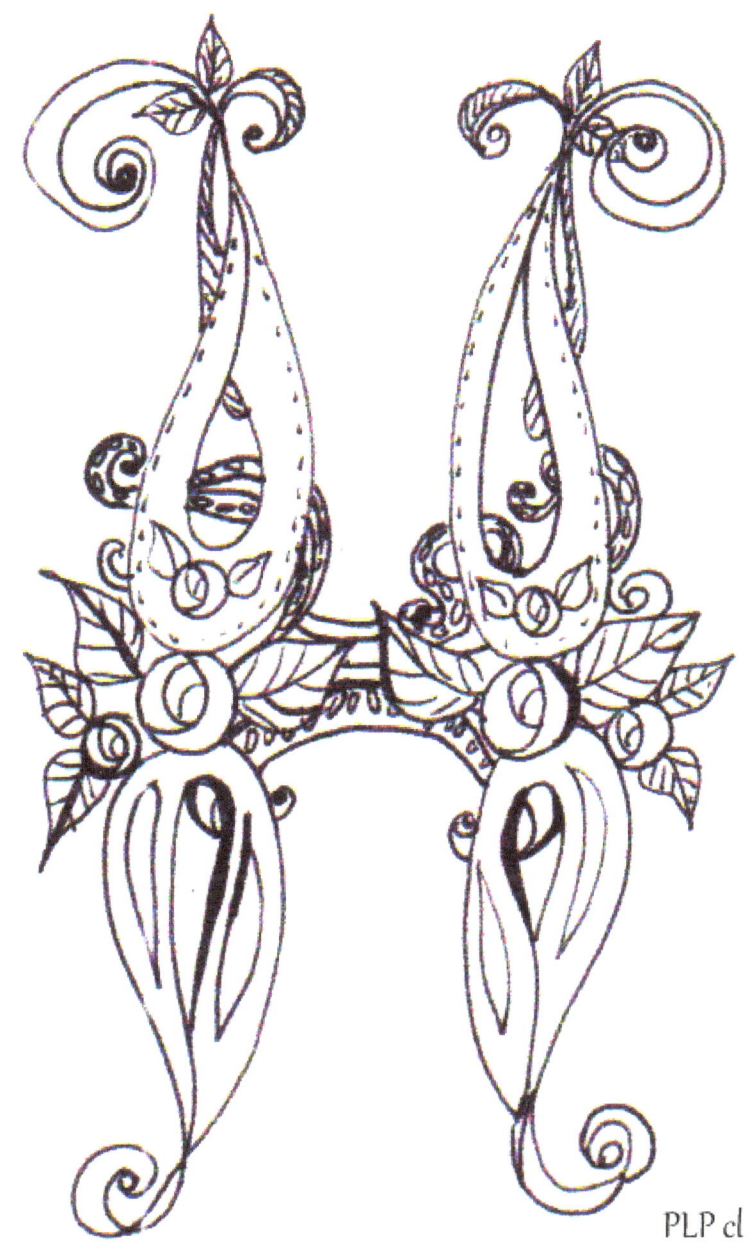

PLP cl

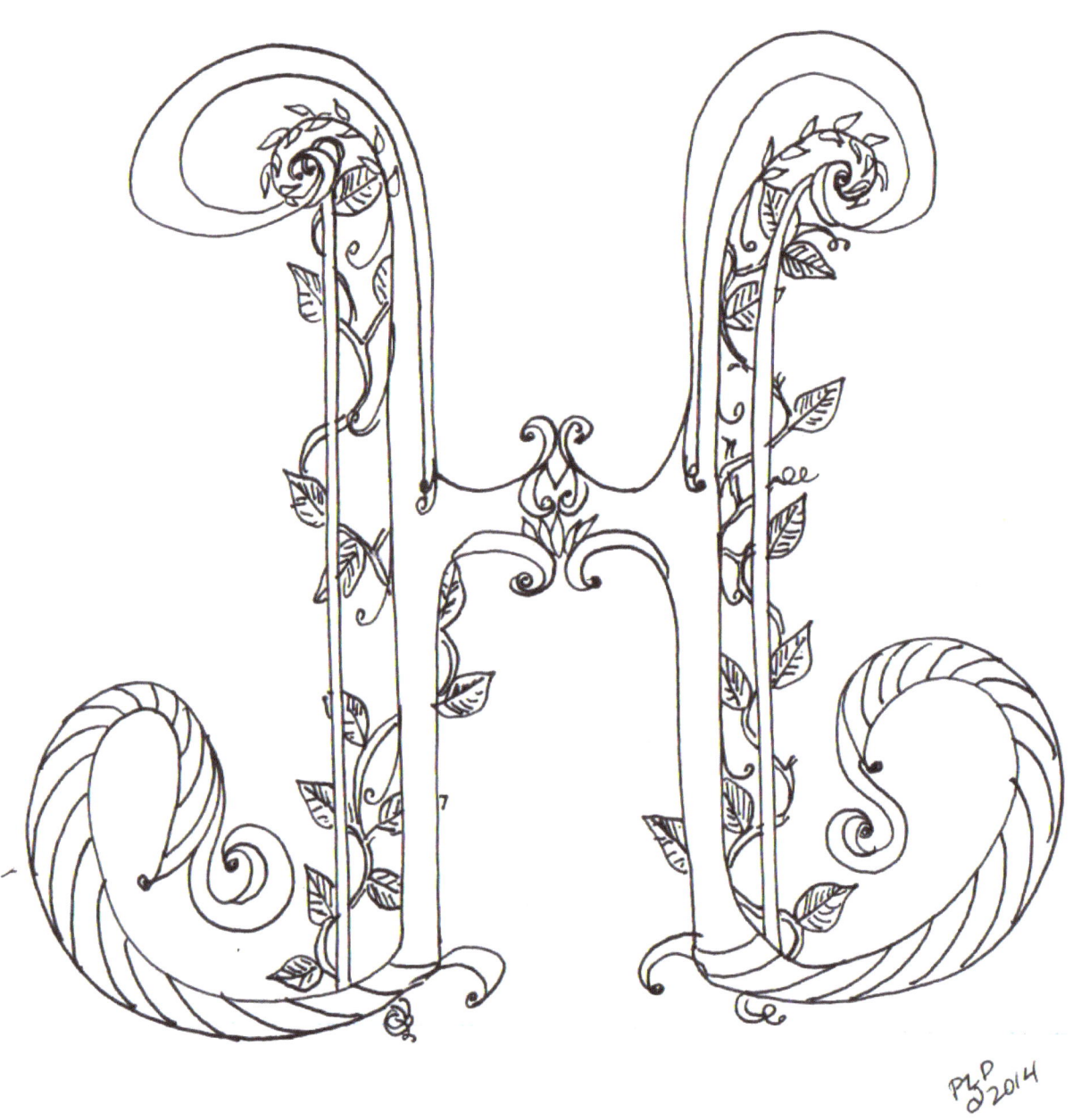

PJP 2014

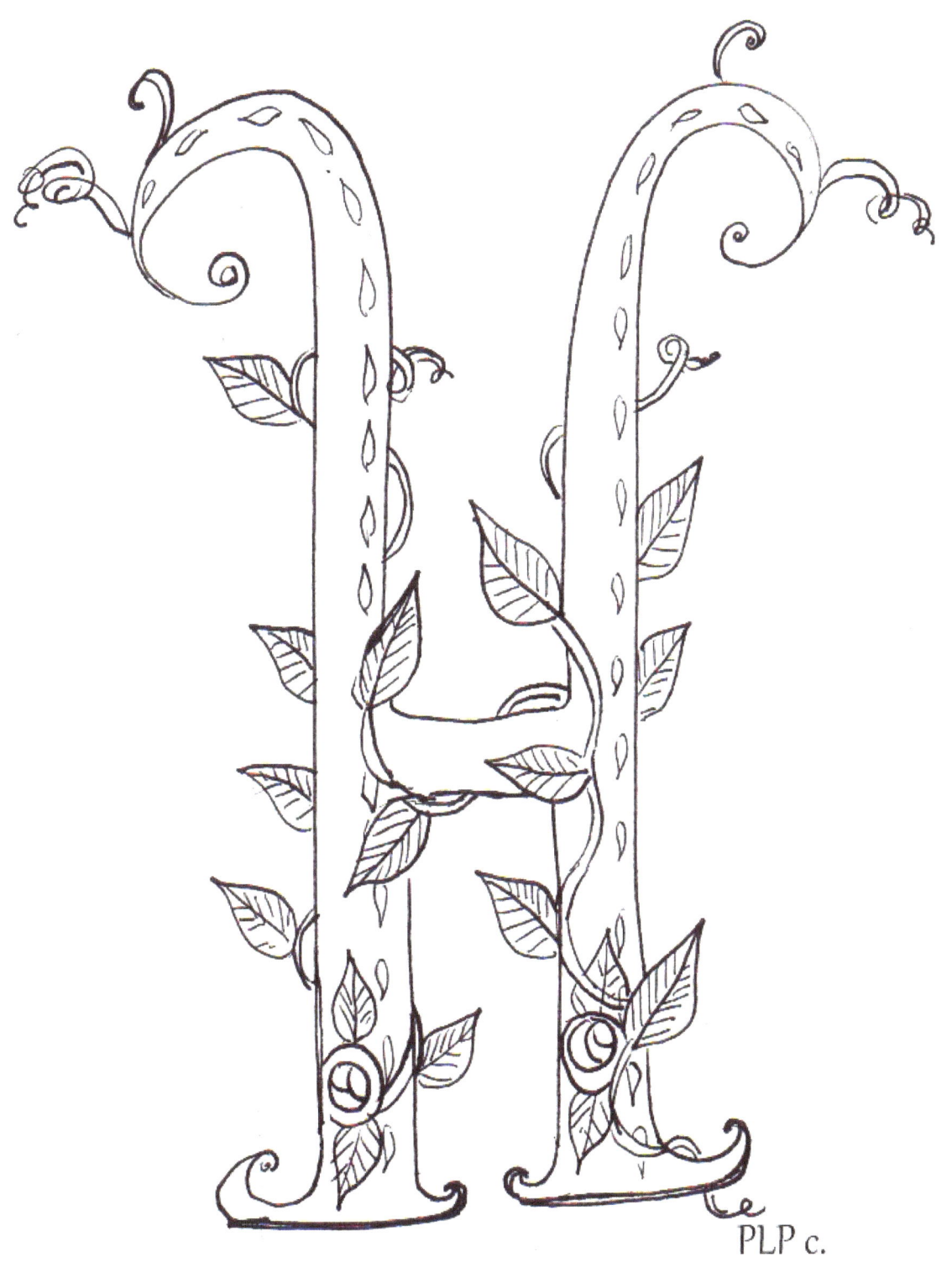

PLP c.

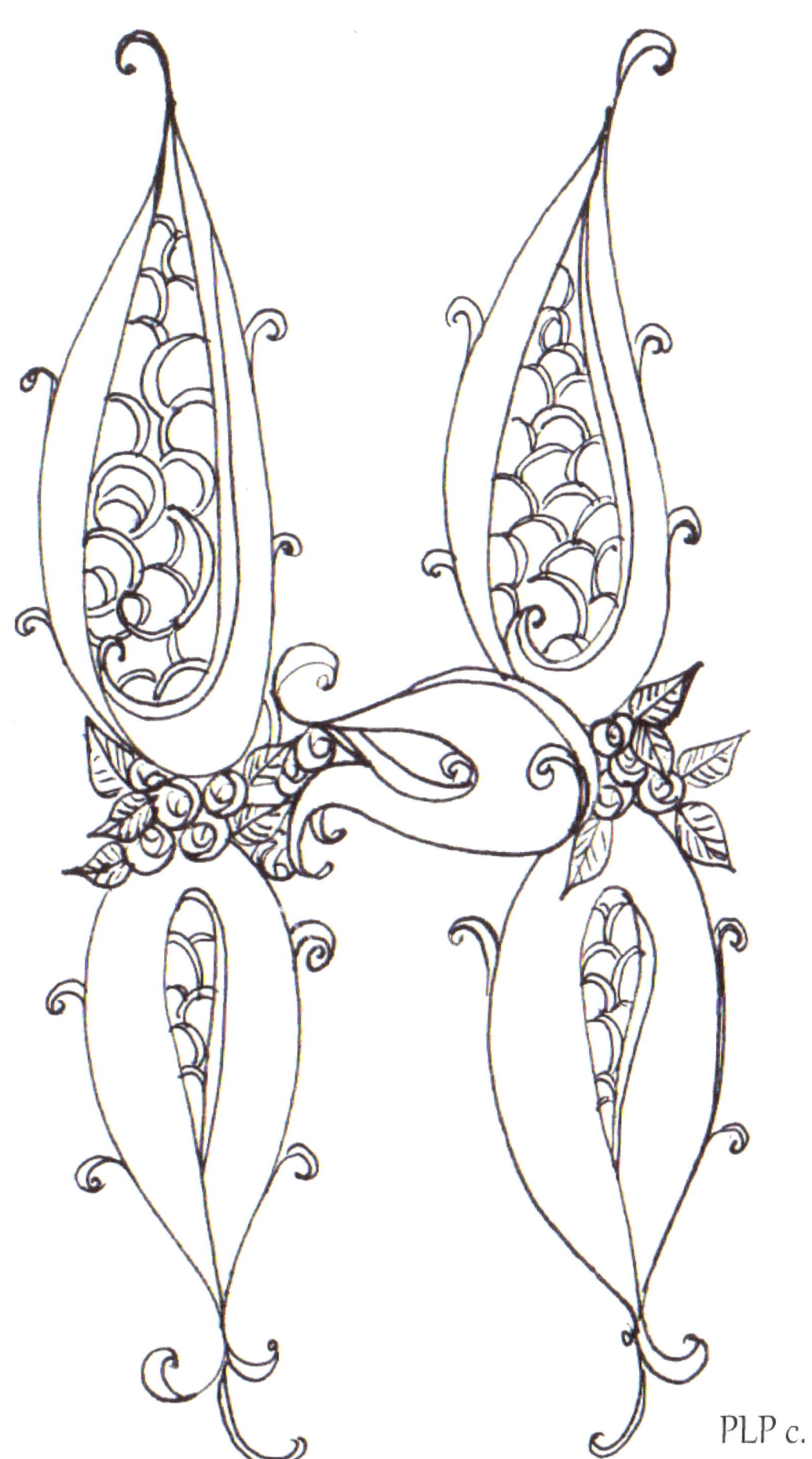

PLP c.

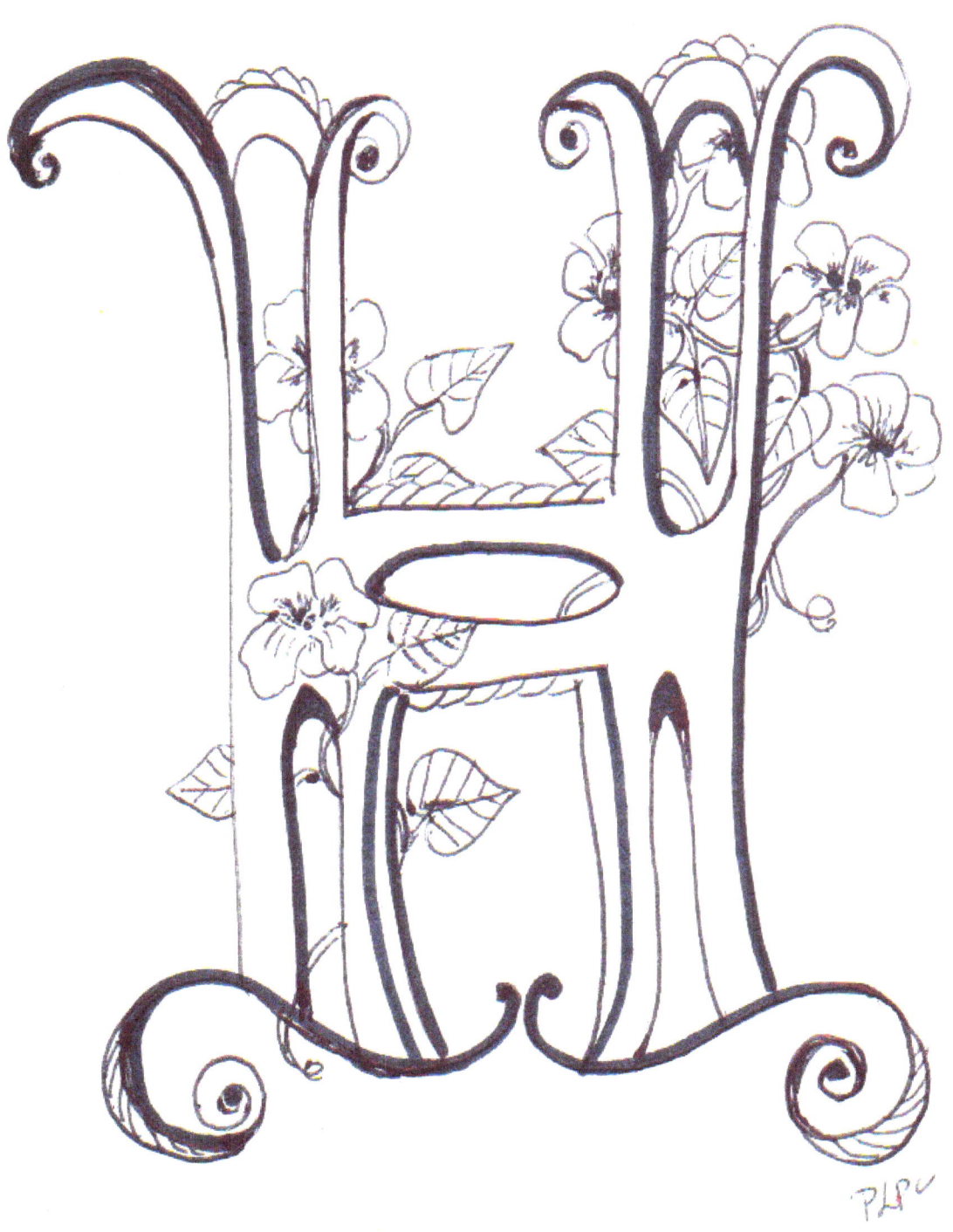

PLP c

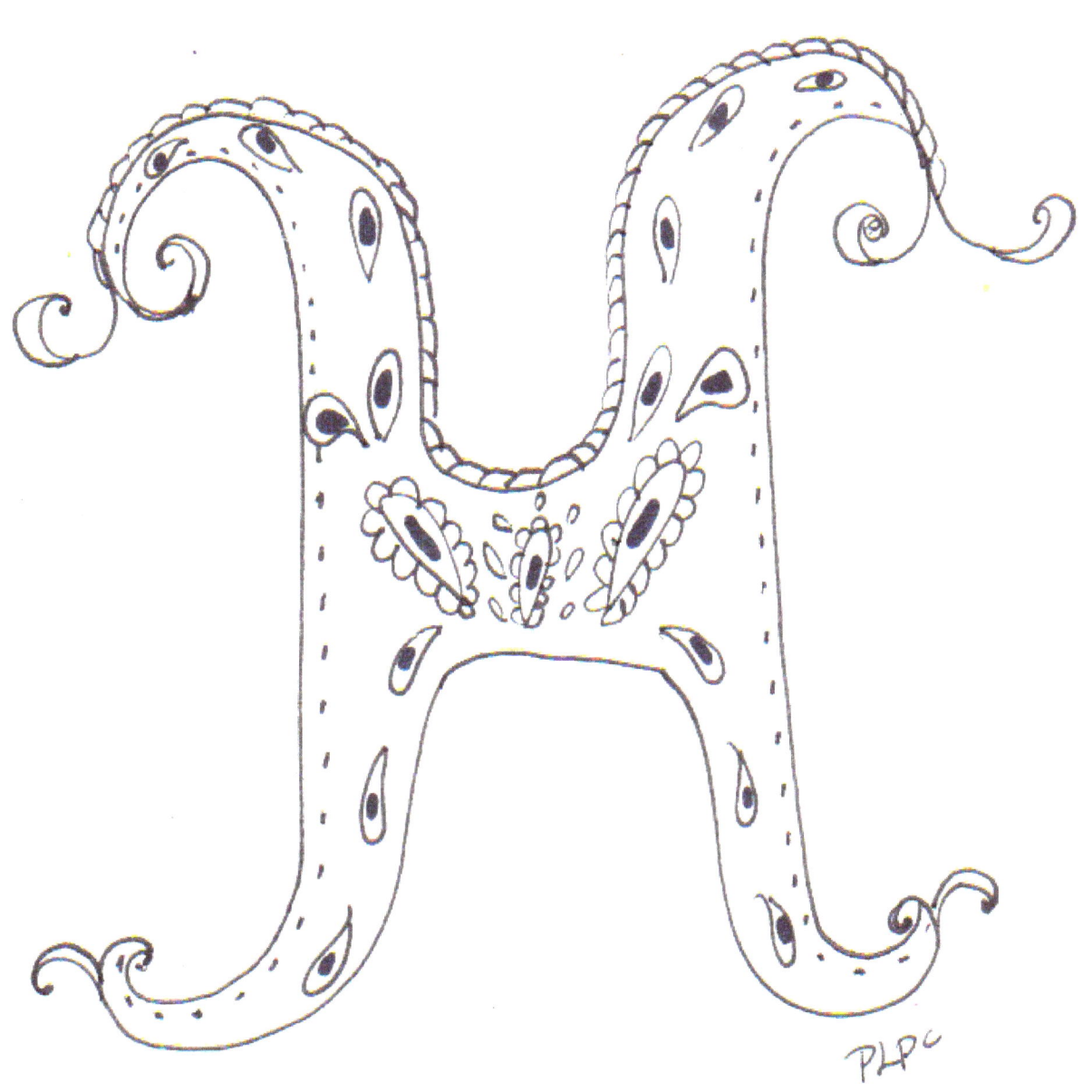

PLPC

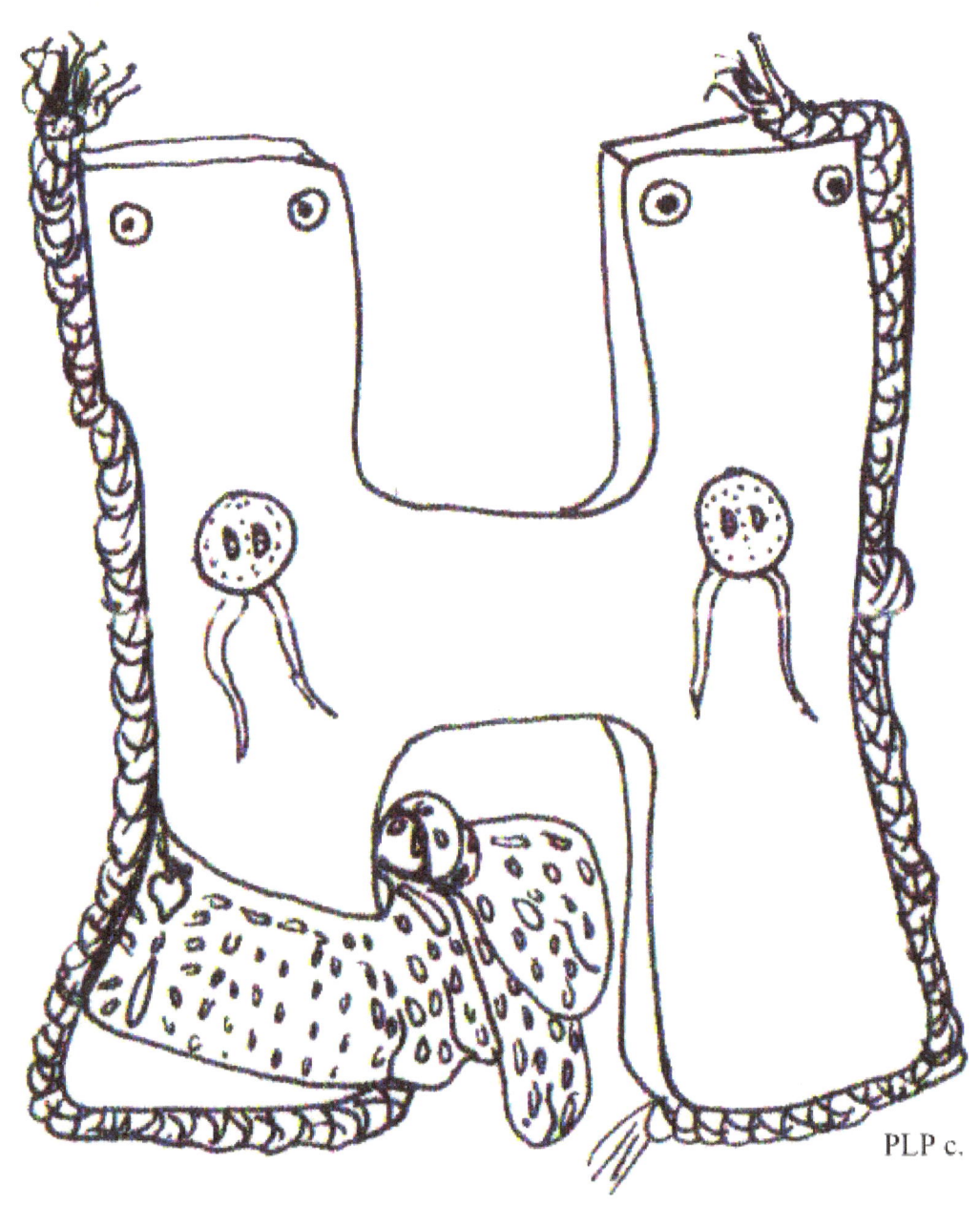

PLP c.

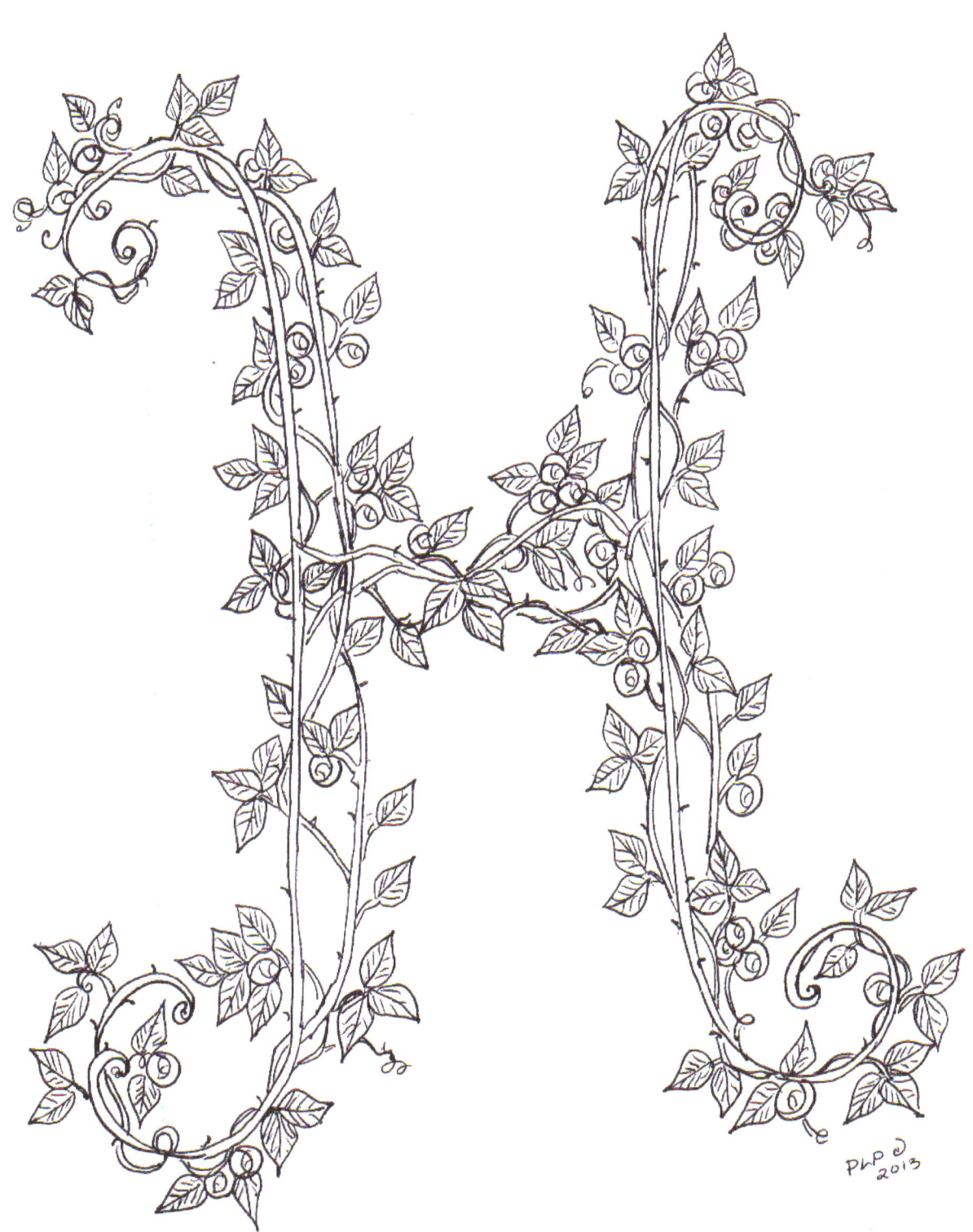

PLP
2013

27

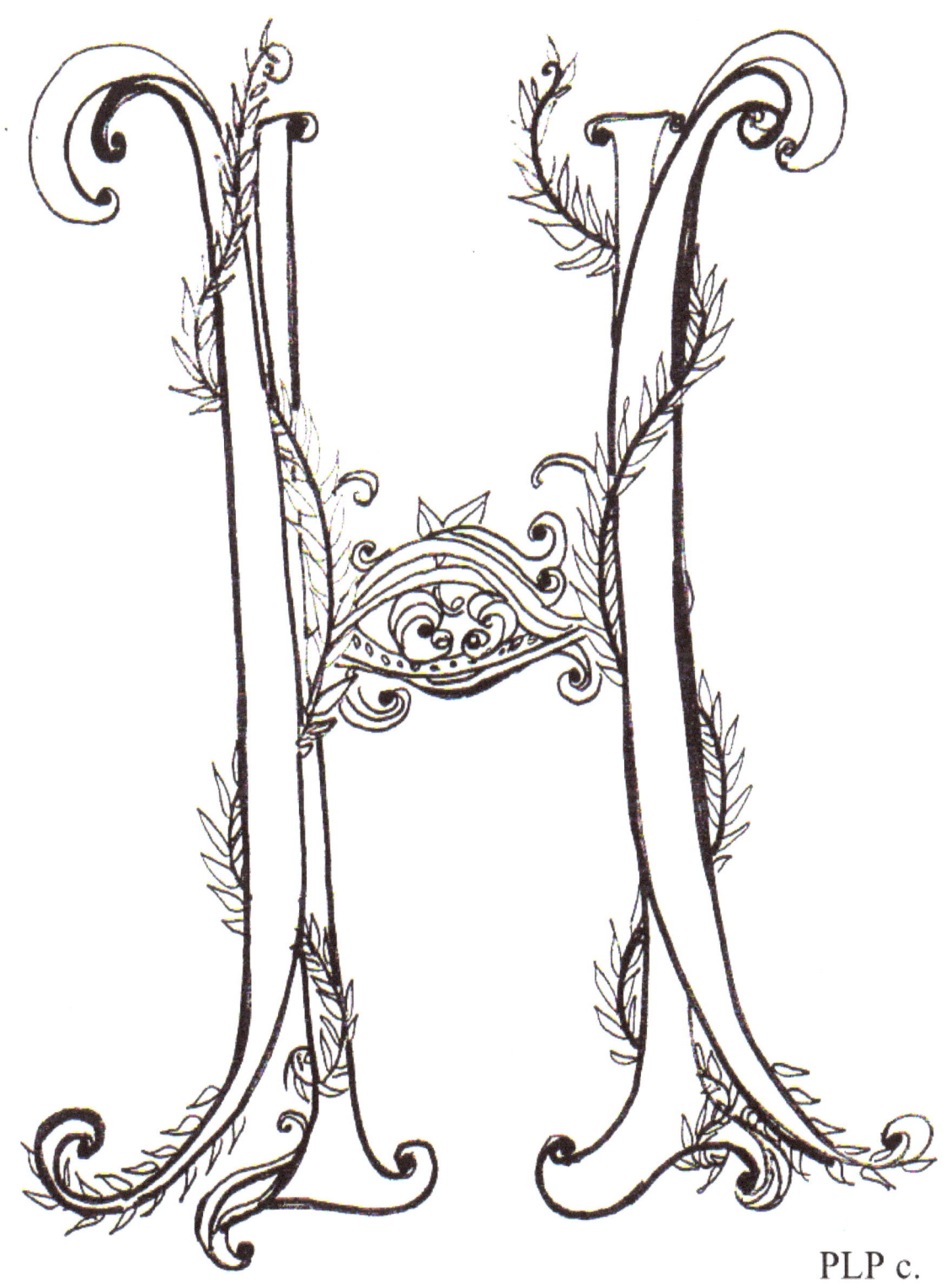

PLP c.

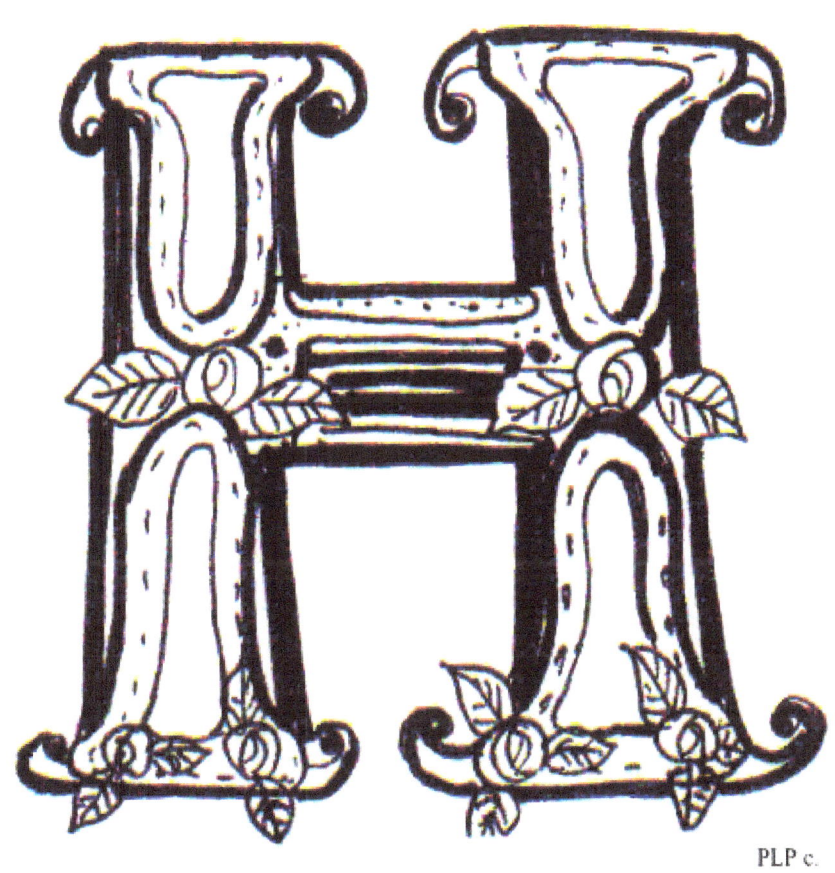

PLP c.

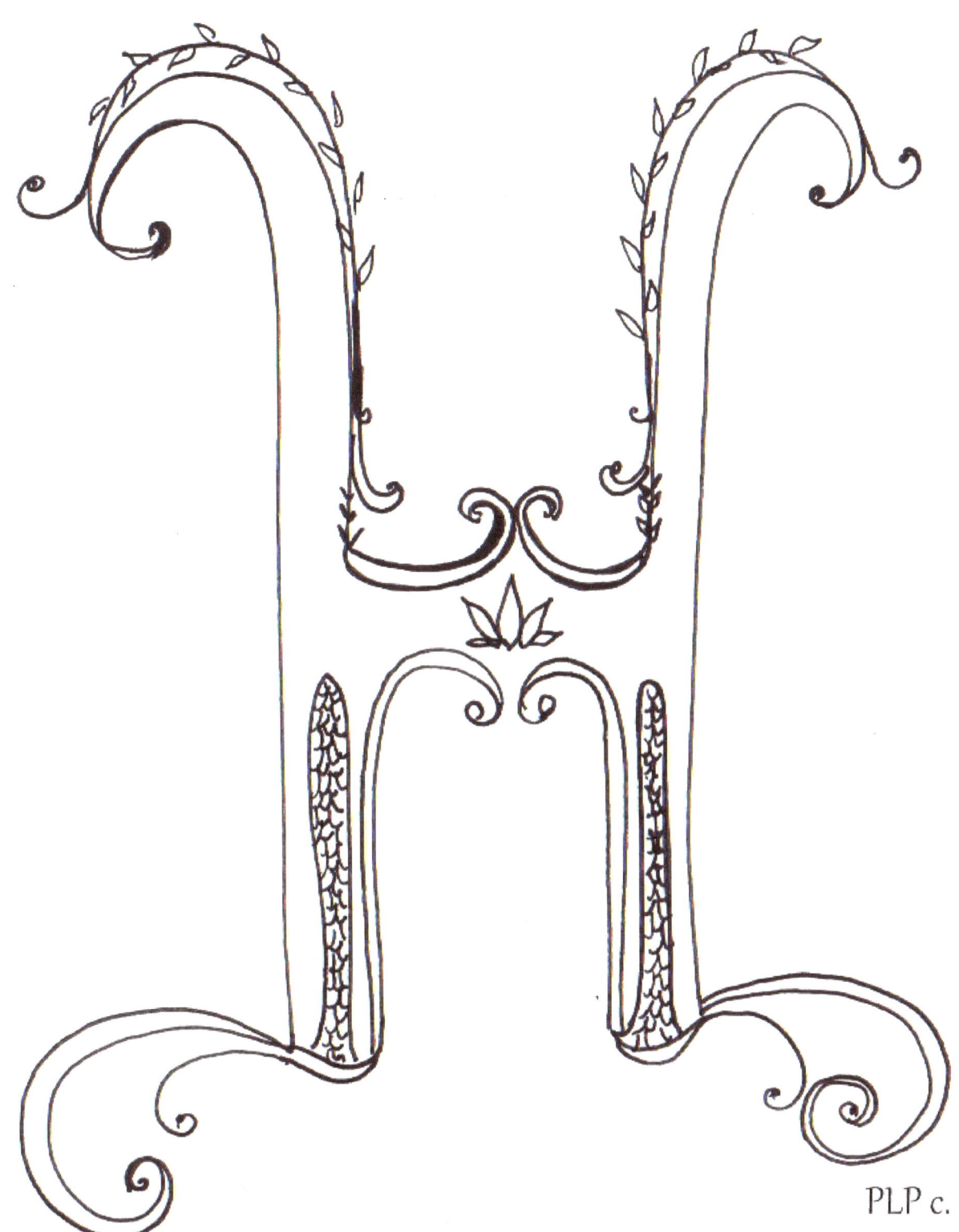

PLP c.

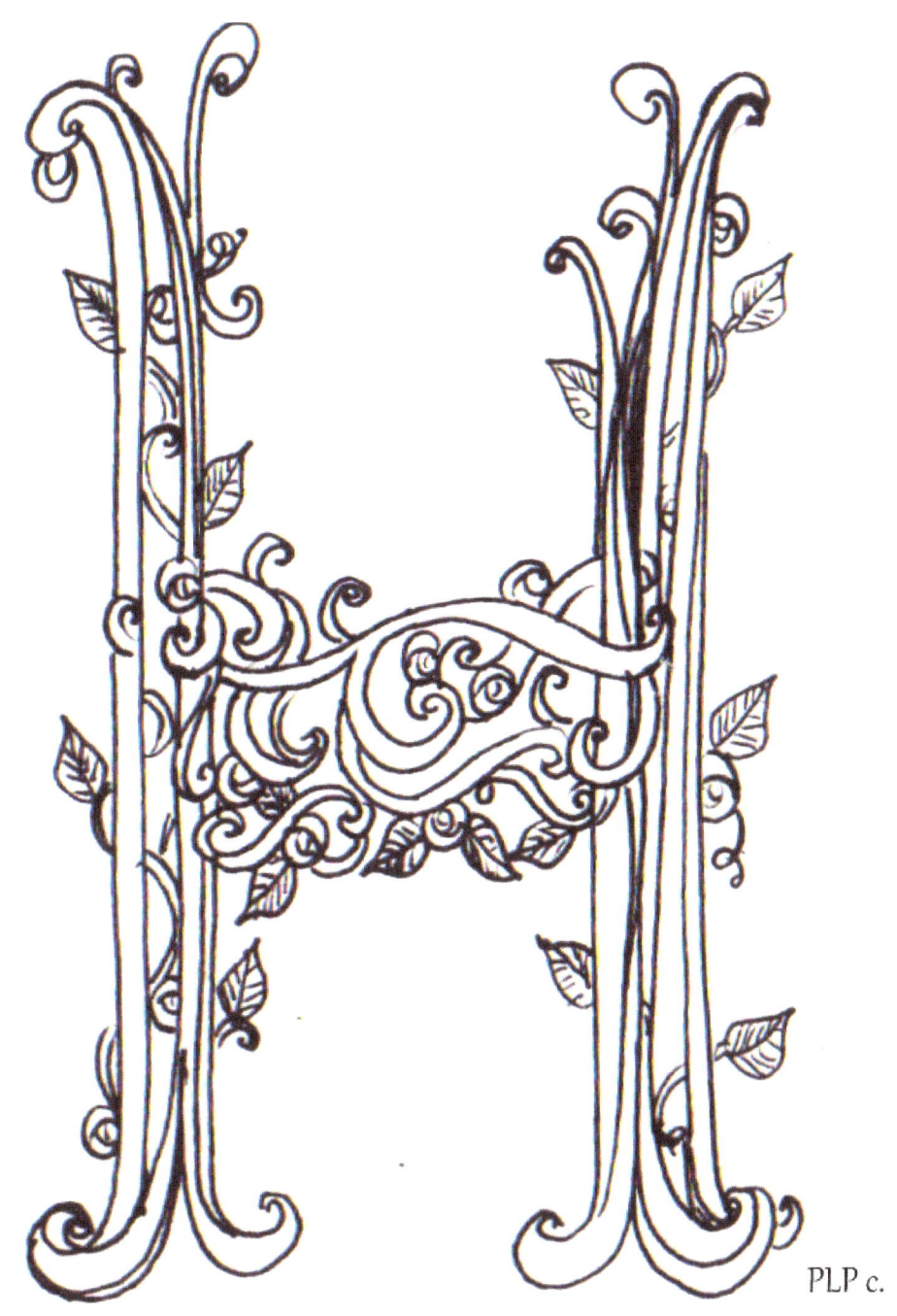

PLP c.

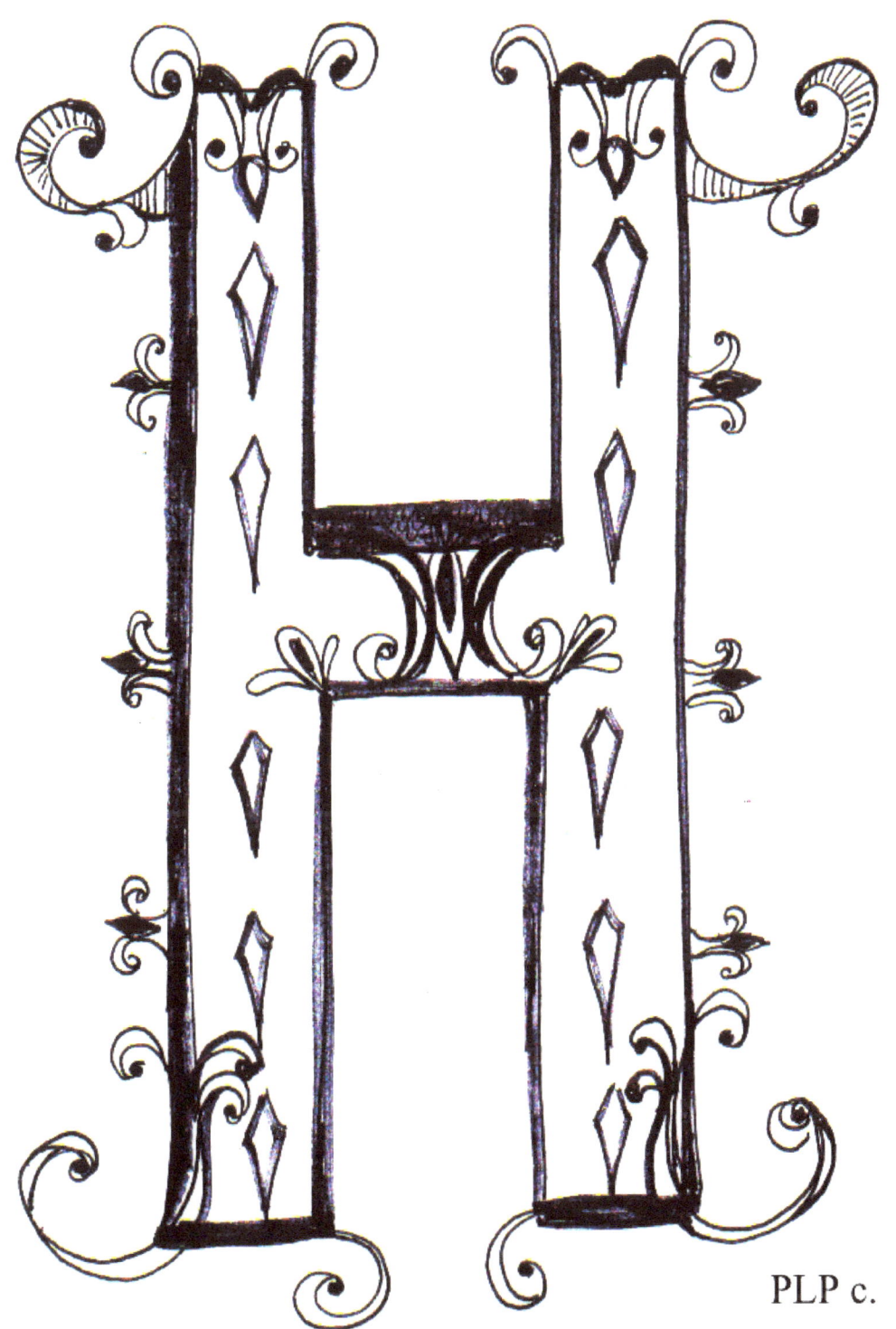

PLP c.

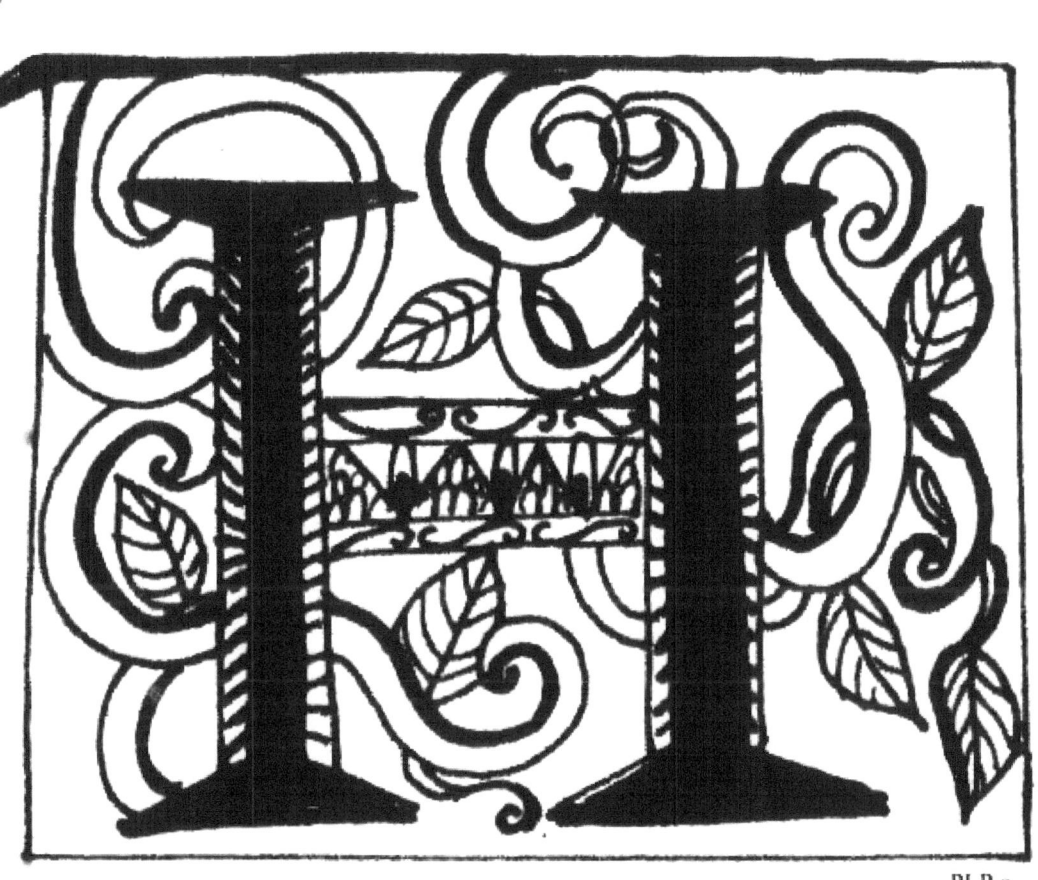

PLP c.

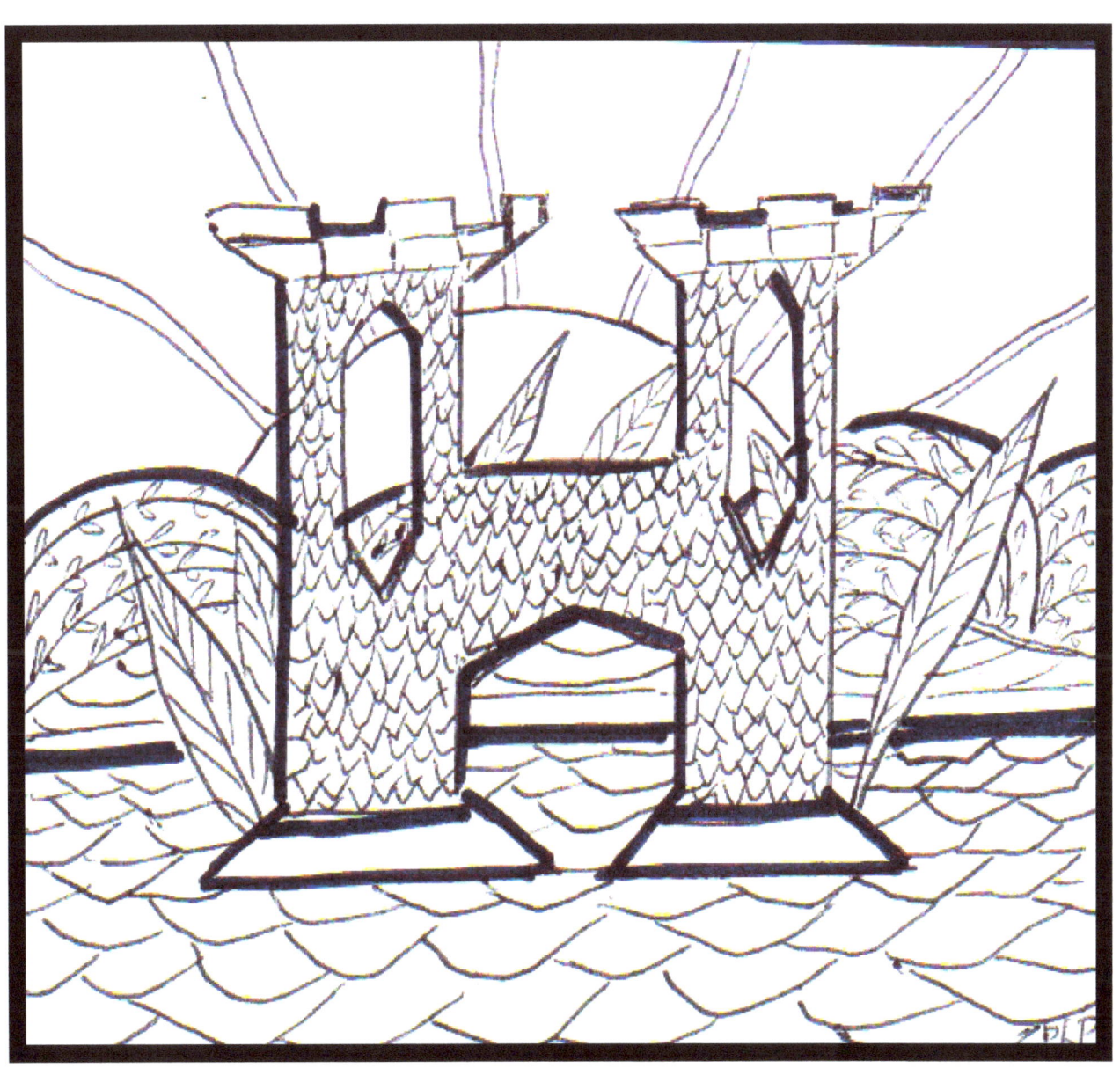

41

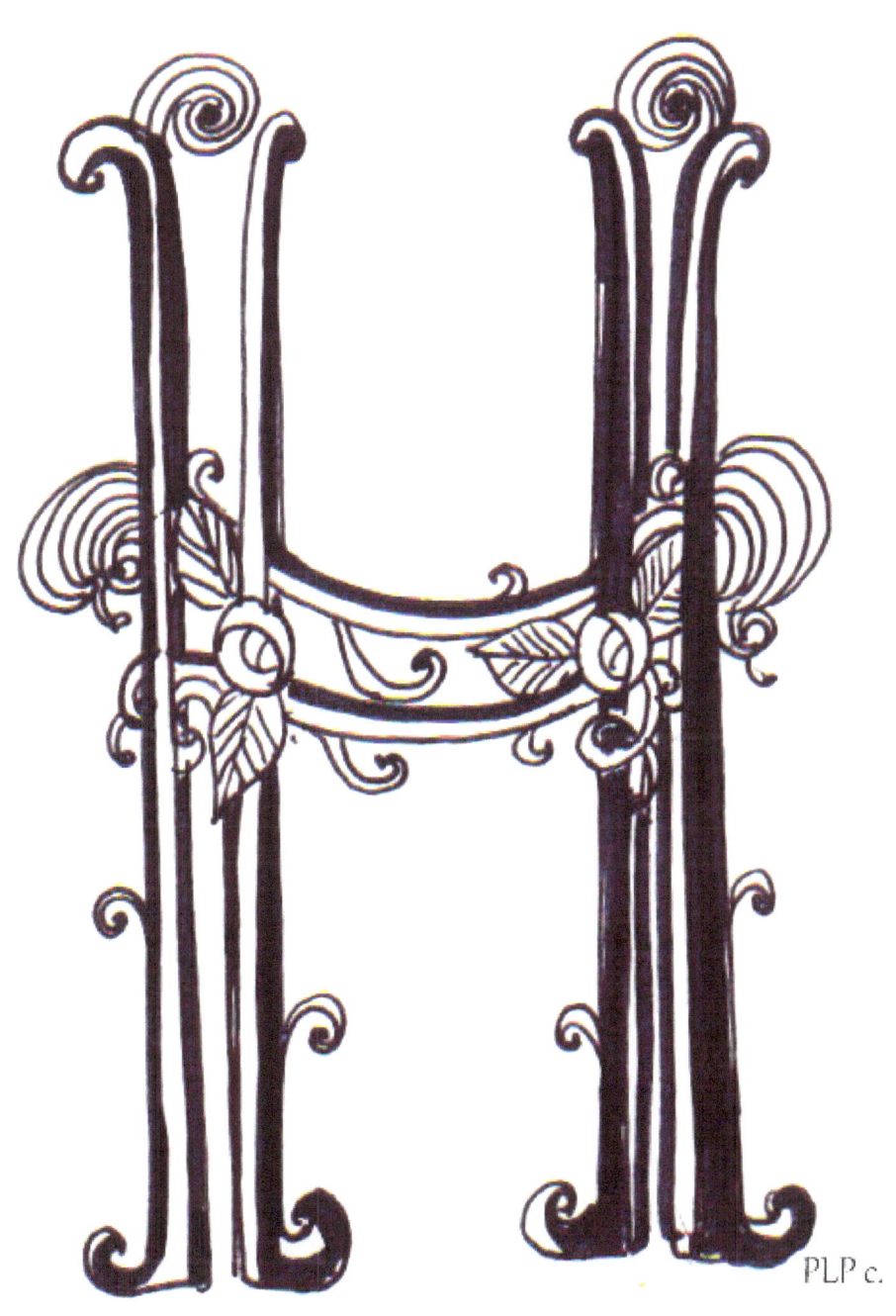

PLP c.

Can you find at least one H in this picture?

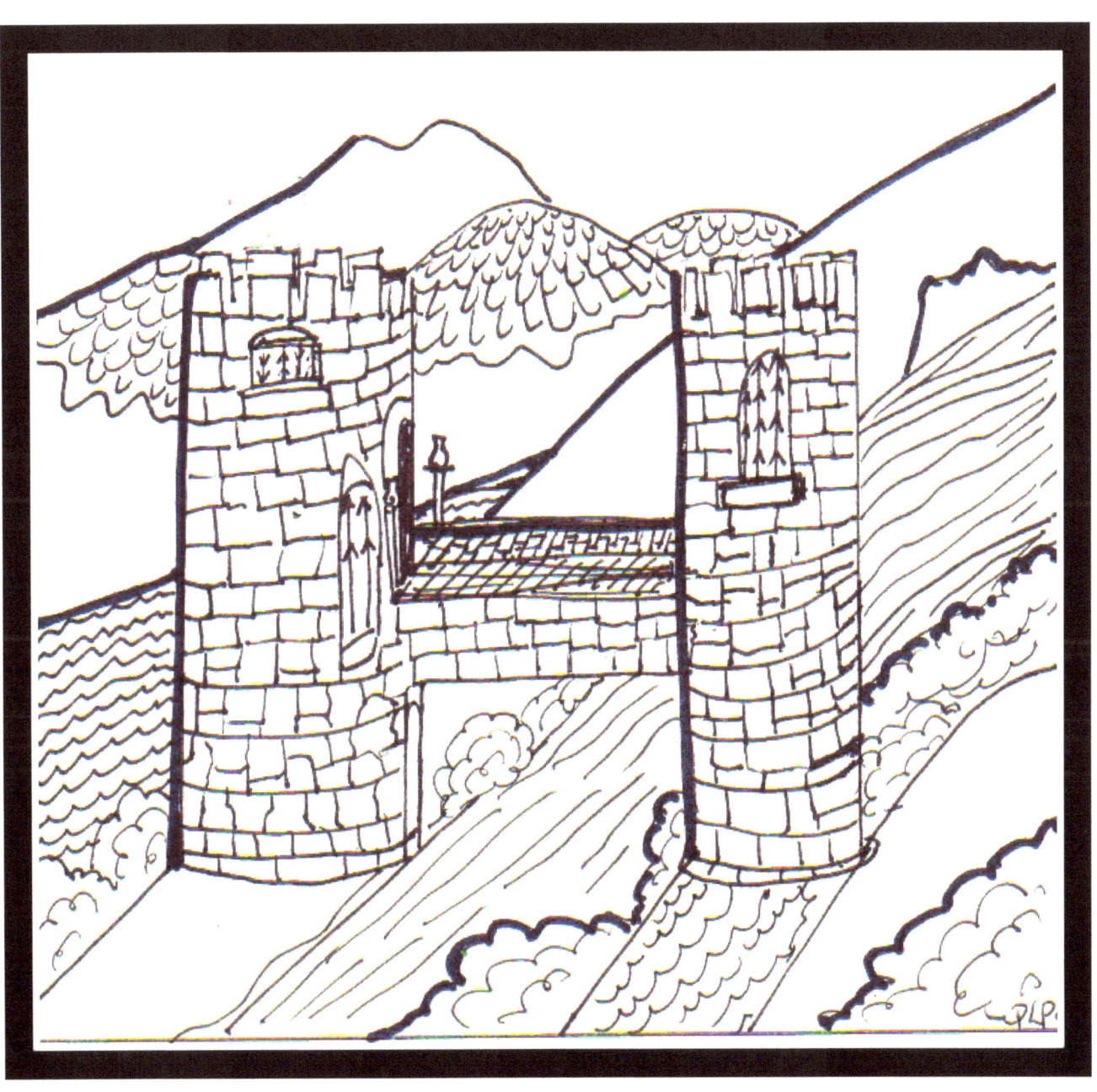

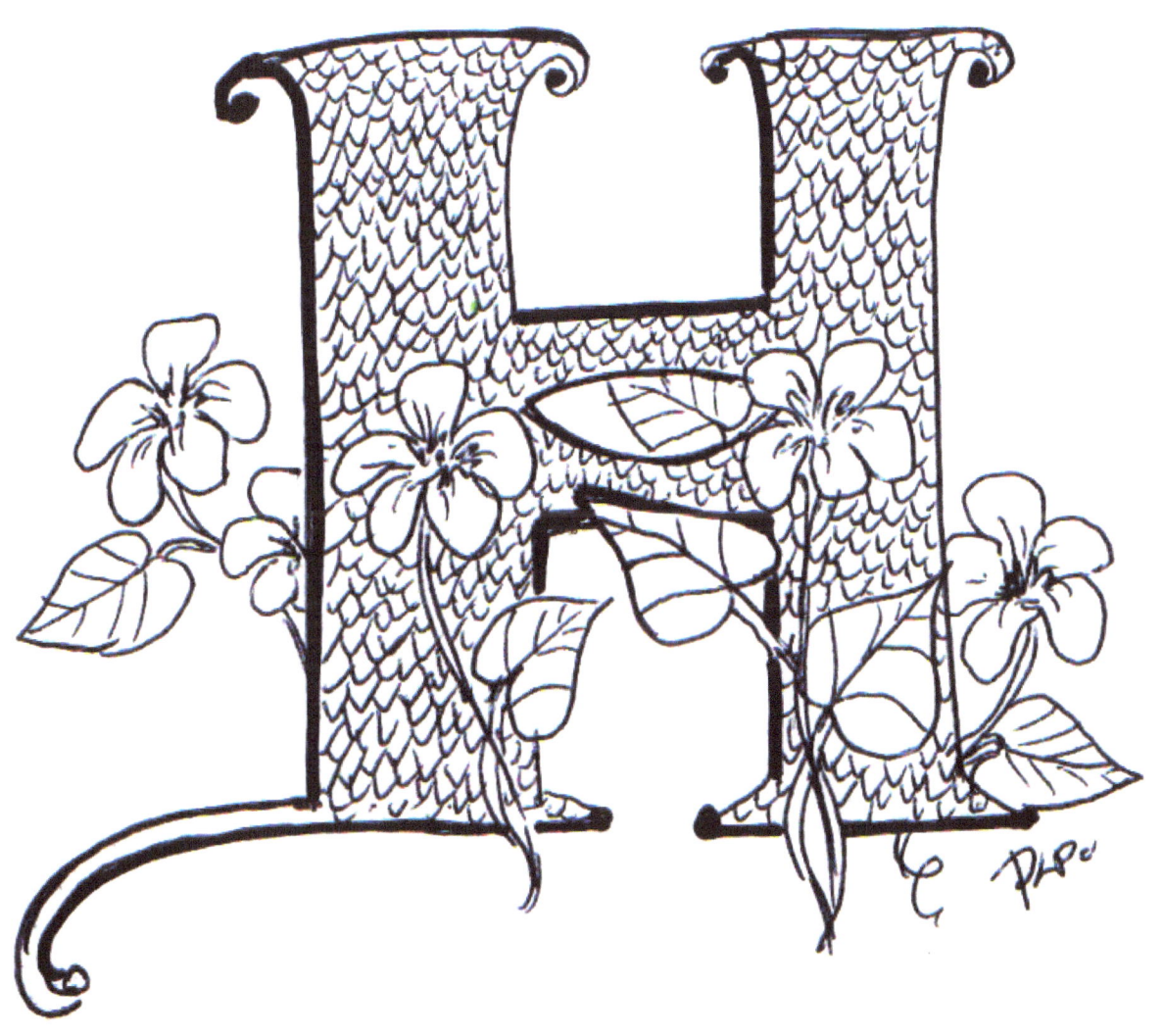

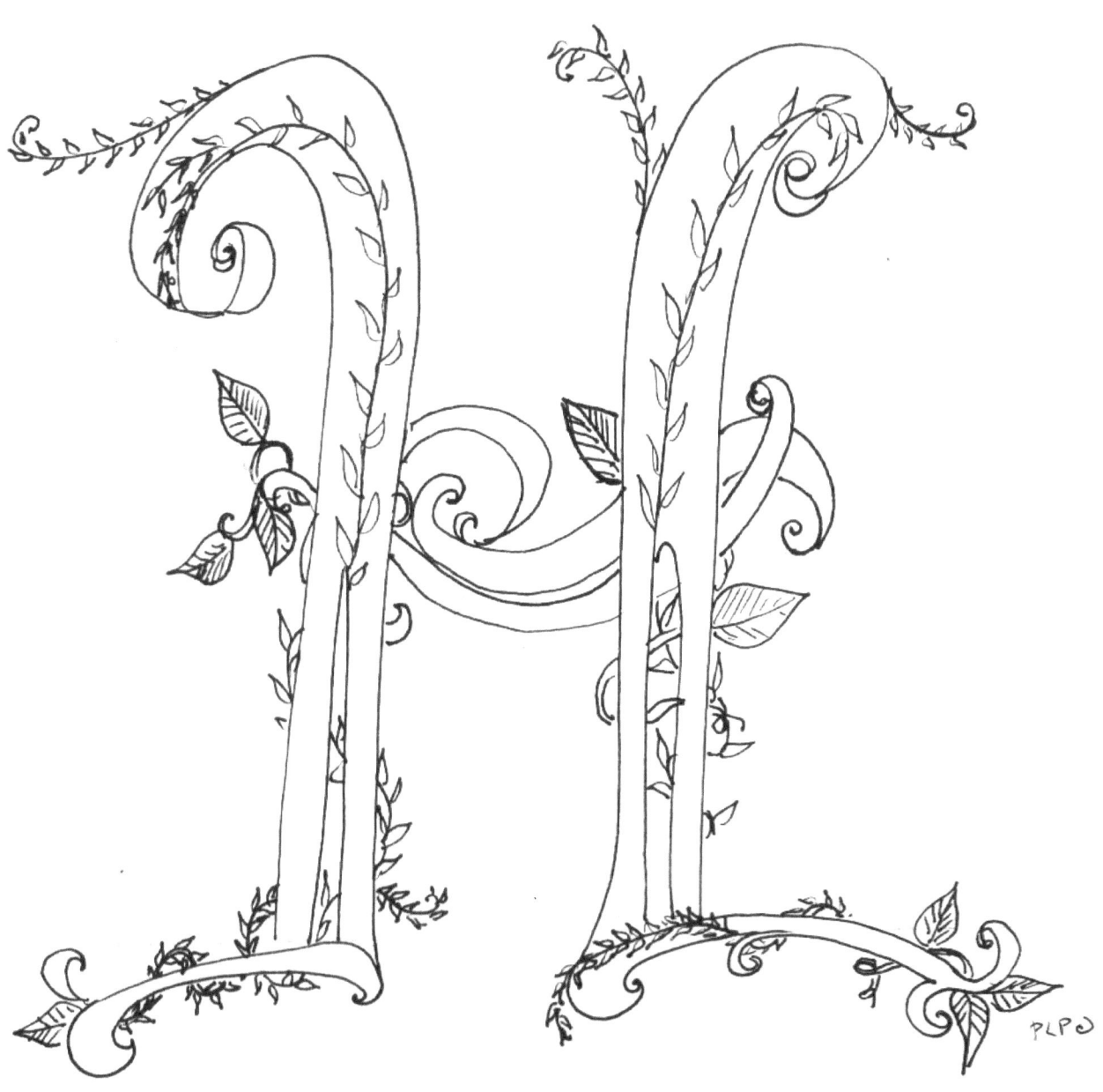

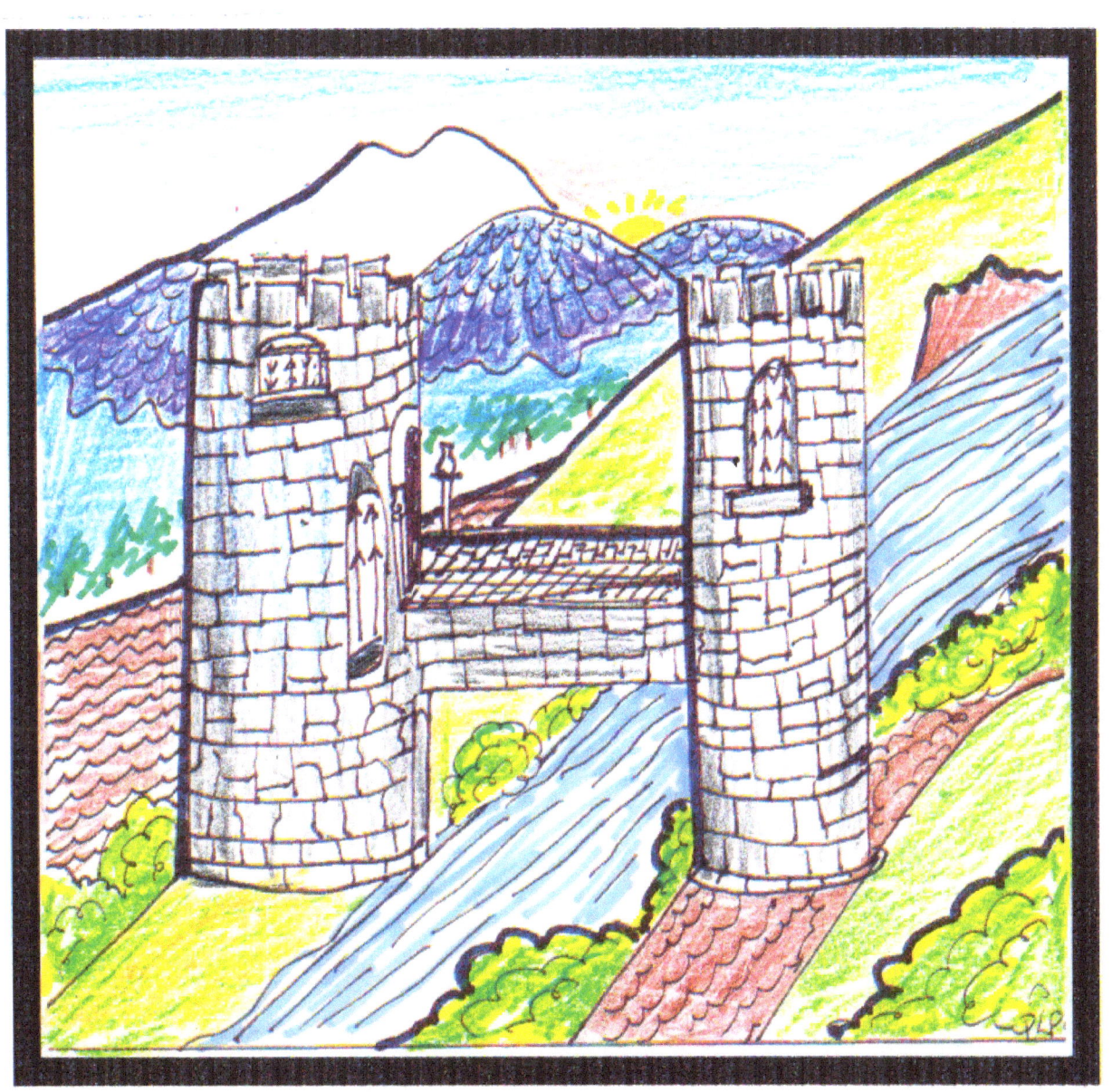

A Letter H can be handsome and very fun!

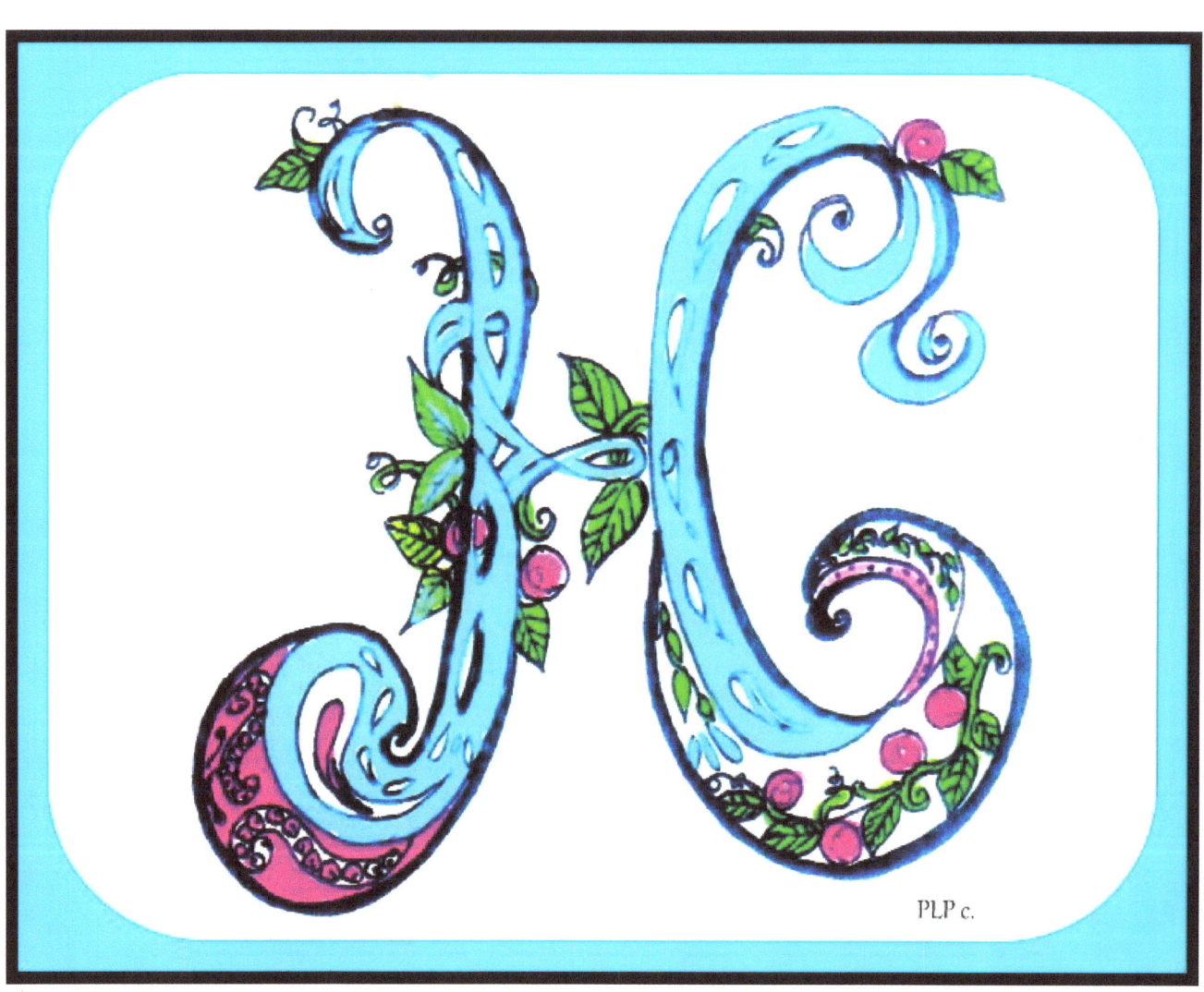

Letter H can travel to far away places.

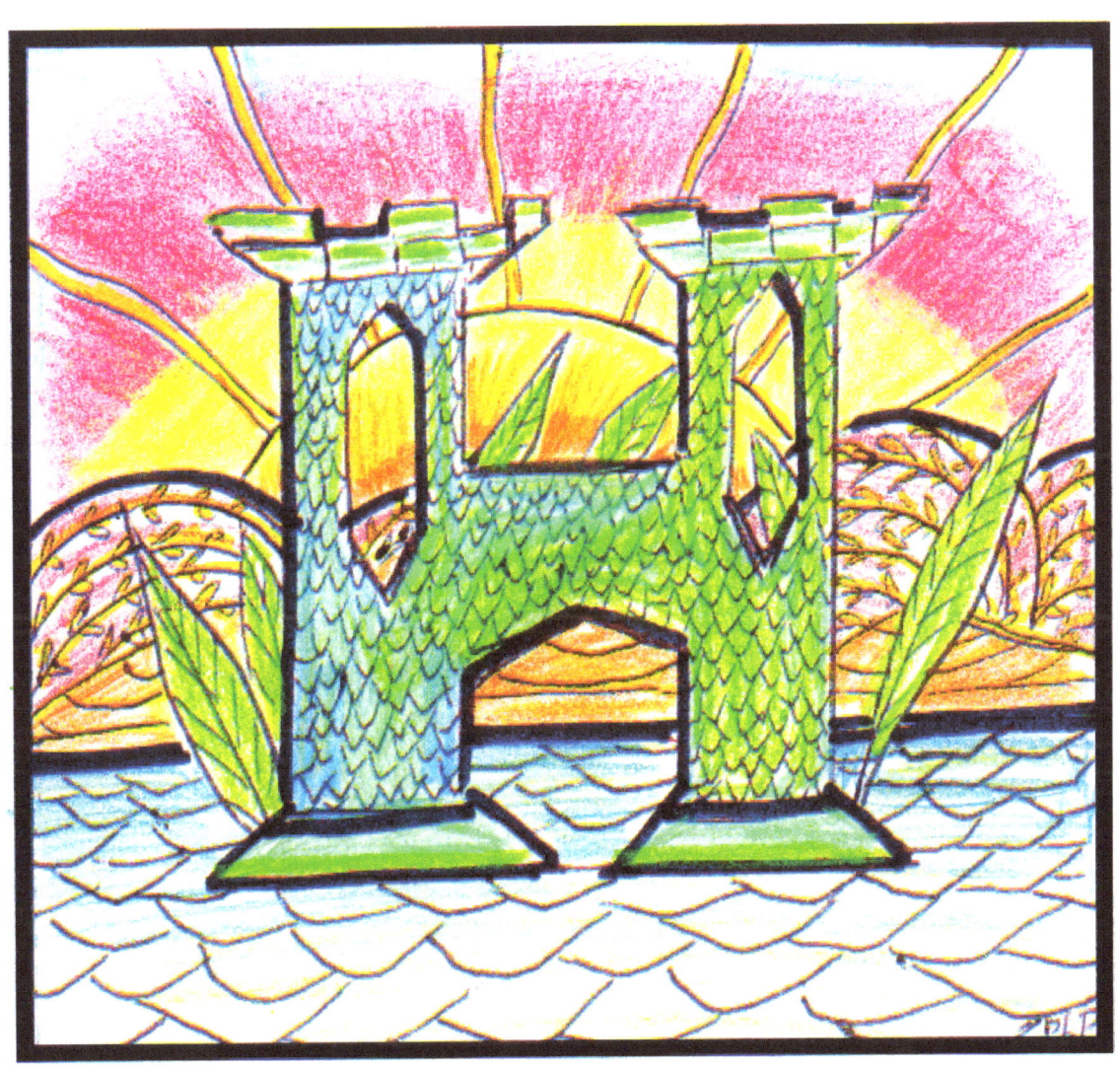

Letter H can have fun in a garden.

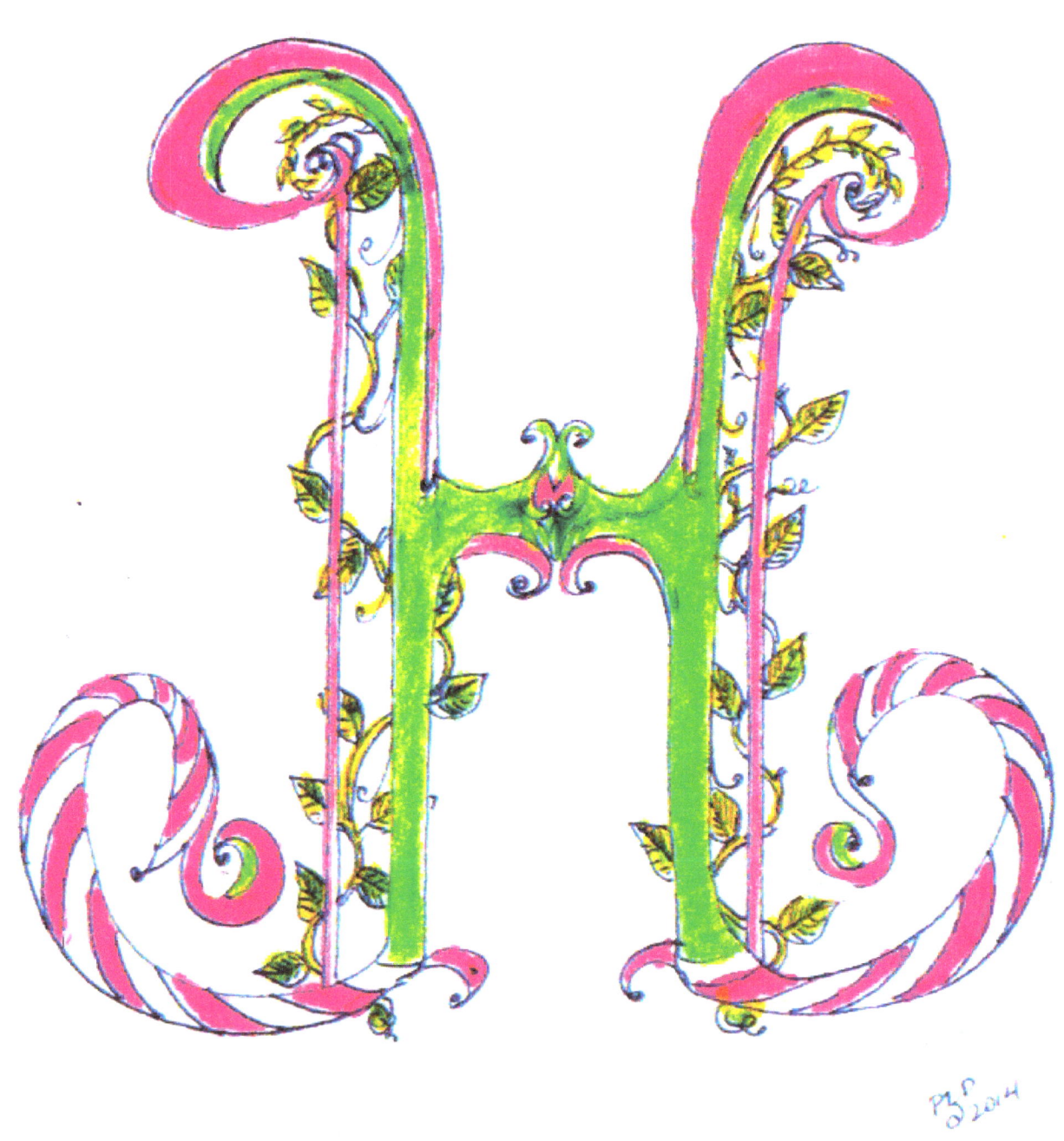

This Handsome H says,

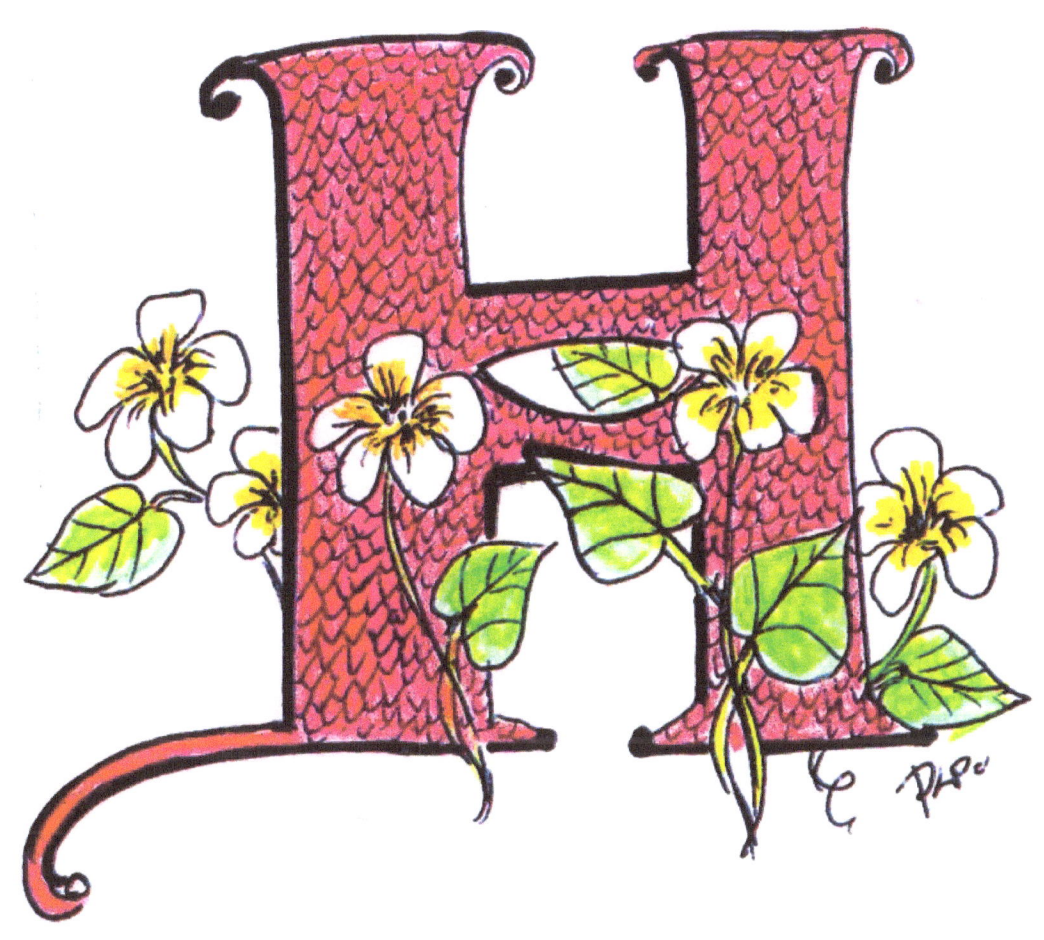

"Hope you had fun Coloring with us. We are

always open to new H designs and colors."